Hop, Frog, Hop!

Written by
Michèle Dufresne

PIONEER VALLEY EDUCATIONAL PRESS, INC.

Look at the **frog**.
The frog can hop.

Hop, frog, hop!

Frogs have long back legs that help them hop.

Look at the frog.
The frog can hop
onto the rock.

Hop, frog, hop!

Frogs can live in water and on land.

Look at the frog.
The frog can hop
onto the log.

Hop, frog, hop!

Look at the big **tree**.

The frog can hop up the tree.

Hop, frog, hop!

The tree frog has sticky disks on its fingers and toes that help it climb.

Look at the big frog.
Frogs do not have **tails.**

8

Baby frogs, called tadpoles, have tails. But their tails disappear as they grow legs.

legs

Look at the frog.

The frog is a mom.

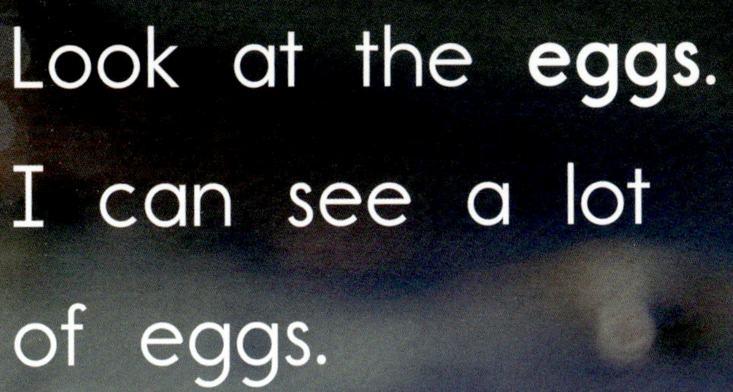

Look at the **eggs.**
I can see a lot
of eggs.

Frogs lay many, many eggs.
When the eggs hatch, they
turn into tadpoles.

glossary

frog

tree

tails

eggs

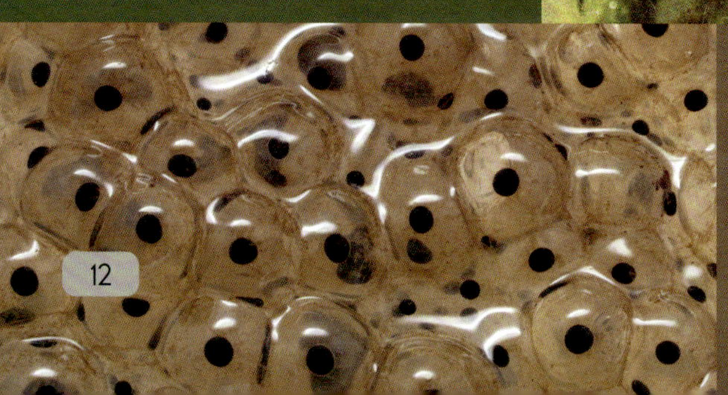